Understanding Business Math & Budgets

Young Adult Library of Small Business and Finance

Young Adult Library of Small Business and Finance

Understanding Business Math & Budgets

Helen Thompson

Mason Crest

Mason Crest
450 Parkway Drive, Suite D
Broomall, PA 19008
www.masoncrest.com

Printed in the United States of America.

First printing
9 8 7 6 5 4 3 2 1

Series ISBN: 978-1-4222-2912-5
ISBN: 978-1-4222-2921-7
ebook ISBN: 978-1-4222-8911-2

The Library of Congress has cataloged the
hardcopy format(s) as follows:

Library of Congress Cataloging-in-Publication Data

Thompson, Helen, 1957-
  Understanding business math & budgets / Helen Thompson.
      pages cm. – (Young adult library of small business and finance)
  Audience: Age 12.
  Audience: Grade 7 to 8.
    ISBN 978-1-4222-2921-7 (hardcover) – ISBN 978-1-4222-2912-5 (series) – ISBN 978-1-4222-8911-2 (ebook)
  1. Business mathematics–Juvenile literature. 2. Budget in business–Juvenile literature. I. Title. II. Title: Understanding business math and budgets.
  HF5691.T474 2014
  510.24'65–dc23
                                    2013016932

Produced by Vestal Creative Services.
www.vestalcreative.com

CONTENTS

INTRODUCTION

Brigitte Madrian, PhD

Small businesses serve a dual role in our economy. They are the bedrock of community life in the United States, providing goods and services that we rely on day in and day out. Restaurants, dry cleaners, car repair shops, plumbers, painters, landscapers, hair salons, dance studios, and veterinary clinics are only a few of the many different types of local small business that are part of our daily lives. Small businesses are also important contributors to the engines of economic growth and innovation. Many of the successful companies that we admire today started as small businesses run out of bedrooms and garages, including Microsoft, Apple, Dell, and Facebook, to name only a few. Moreover, the founders of these companies were all very young when they started their firms. Great business ideas can come from people of any age. If you have a great idea, perhaps you would like to start your own small business. If so, you may be wondering: What does it take to start a business? And how can I make my business succeed?

A successful small business rests first and foremost on a great idea—a product or service that other people or businesses want and are willing to pay for. But a good idea is not enough. Successful businesses start with a plan. A business plan defines what the business will do, who its customers will be, where the firm will be located, how the firm will market the company's product, who the firm will hire, how the business will be financed, and what, if any, are the firm's plans for future growth. If a firm needs a loan from a bank in order to start up, the bank will mostly likely want to see a written business plan. Writing a business plan helps an entrepreneur think

Introduction

through all the possible road blocks that could keep a business from succeeding and can help convince a bank to make a loan to the firm.

Once a firm has the funding in place to open shop, the next challenge is to connect with the firm's potential customers. How will potential customers know that the company exists? And how will the firm convince these customers to purchase the company's product? In addition to finding customers, most successful businesses, even small ones, must also find employees. What types of employees should a firm hire? And how much should they be paid? How do you motivate employees to do their jobs well? And what do you do if employees don't get along? Managing employees is an important skill in running almost any successful small business.

Finally, firms must also understand the rules and regulations that govern how they operate their business. Some rules, like paying taxes, apply to all businesses. Other rules apply to only certain types of firms. Does the firm need a license to operate? Are there restrictions on where the firm can locate or when it can be open? What other regulations must the firm comply with?

Starting up a small business is a lot of work. But despite the hard work, most small business owners find their jobs

Understanding Business Math & Budgets

rewarding. While many small business owners are happy to have their business stay small, some go on to grow their firms into more than they ever imagined, big companies that service customers throughout the world.

What will your small business do?

Brigitte Madrian, PhD
Aetna Professor of Public Policy and Corporate Management
Harvard Kennedy School

Introduction

9

ONE

Math and Business

Lots of young people groan at the thought of math class, wondering why they will ever need what they're learning. "Percentages *again*?!" you might say in math class. Or, "I'll never use fractions in real life."

But you will, in fact, need plenty of the things you're learning in math class. You'll use percentages to figure out sales in stores, and you'll use fractions to cook. You may use math in some way every day of your life!

Even though programs like Excel do some of the math for you, understanding business math will make using programs like this much easier.

If you ever start a business, you will find yourself using math all the time. Or if you're already running a business, that's a lesson you may have already learned.

If you understand math, that will help your business a lot. You'll be able to keep track of how much money you're making. You can decide whether you should offer sales to customers. You'll even be able to figure out whether your business is successful—all with math.

 **Understanding Business Math & Budgets**

What Kind of Math Will I Need?

Most of the math you will use in business is pretty simple. You will need to know how to add, subtract, multiply, and divide. You will also need to understand percentages and fractions. Beyond that, you may need to use a few slightly more complicated equations.

What is really important is knowing *when* to use which kind of math. You should be able to look at your business **receipts** and know exactly what you need to do to see if you have spent too much money on your business. And you should be able to keep track of your business's money without confusing all the numbers.

Think of business math as a bunch of word problems. In school, you're used to reading a paragraph about a situation where you have to use math. With business math, you're actually living the word problem!

MATH TOOLS

Although being able to do math in your head is a good skill to have, you can also use some tools when you're doing business math. Calculators are one sort of tool you can use to do calculations. Excel (a software program) is another great tool, especially for business math. Excel lets you keep all your math in one place, on a spreadsheet. You can do calculations right in Excel. You can even make charts out of your information, which makes the math easier to see. Play around with Excel and learn about everything it can do for you.

You might find it helpful to actually write down the math you're using. Make your real-life word problem into a paragraph so you can see what's going on. After a while, you'll get used to the sorts of math problems you have to deal with in business, and they'll get easier.

Practice Makes Perfect

Don't worry if you're not great at math. You're used to learning math in school, doing worksheets and tests. You might find you understand math a lot better when you're actually using it outside of class. It may start to make sense to you when you see how it applies to real life.

OTHER BUSINESS SKILLS

Besides math, business people have plenty of other skills that help them along the way. Business owners are often creative. If you run your own business, you have to come up with products and services to sell, advertisements, and more. Customer service skills are also important when it comes to business. You want to be friendly and helpful when working with customers, or else no one will want to buy anything from you! Another skill business owners should have is organization. Businesses have a lot going on, and you need to be able to keep track of everything. Receipts, customer orders, and budgets are just some of the things you'll need to keep organized.

Understanding Business Math & Budgets

Pay attention to the times you have to use math when doing business. If you're at the grocery store, and you notice **unit price** on the price labels, try to figure out what the numbers mean. If you can't quite understand them, go home and do a little research. You won't be tested on your knowledge, so it's okay if it takes you a while to really understand what you're looking at.

Ask for help if you need it. Plenty of people would be happy to help. Ask your family for some math help, or friends who love math. You could also ask your math teacher at school for help. She will probably be very happy to help a student with a real-life math problem.

The more you notice and start to practice math, the easier it will get. Even if you already really like math and have a good understanding of it, keep practicing. You can always improve your math skills! Business is a perfect place to practice.

TWO

Keeping Track of the Money

Most of the business math you will work with has to do with money. You will need to calculate how much your business is spending and how much it is making.

Not only do you have to do the math, you have to keep track of it. Doing a calculation once and then forgetting the answer won't do you any good. You have to put that answer somewhere, preferably with a lot of other answers. Keeping track of your business money is called bookkeeping.

Businesses use money every day. Let's say you have just started a t-shirt business. You want to create t-shirts that your friends and other customers will want to buy. You have come up with a few designs, and you have small t-shirt press you bought online to start your business. You already have money to keep track of, and you haven't even started selling any t-shirts!

You think ahead to when your business is a little bigger. Money will come in when customers buy t-shirts. You will have to buy more t-shirts and advertisements. In the future, your business may have borrowed money from individuals or the bank, and you will have to pay it back. You may have to pay employees (and yourself). You need to save money to buy things for your business in the future. That's a lot of money to keep track of!

A good system for keeping track of your money goes a long way toward a good business. You'll know what is happening with the money in your business. Otherwise, you may lose some of it or put your company out of business.

Physical Files

You'll have a lot of papers once you get your business up and running. Receipts, check stubs, notes, and your business plan will all need a place so you don't lose any of those documents.

Set up a filing system. Keep a folder for each type of paper you have. Have one folder for bank statements, one for sales information, one for *expense* information, and one for advertisement examples. Each folder should have just one kind of file in it. Filing makes finding what you need a lot easier.

Have a filing cabinet where you keep all your folders. Label each folder clearly, so you can easily find the one you're looking for right when you need it. The better organized you are, the less frustrated you'll be when you need to look at paperwork.

Keep your physical files for seven years. Consider putting the most important documents in a fireproof box, so they are safe from harm no matter what happens.

YOUR BUSINESS PLAN

One of your most important files is your business plan. Every business needs a map of where it's going and how it will get there. That map is called a business plan. Your business plan should include:

- a description of your business, along with your goals and the reasons why your business exists.
- a marketing plan, which describes how you'll get customers to buy what you're selling. Marketing includes advertising, packaging, and places you will sell.
- a description of your competition.
- a section on how you will organize and manage your business, including any employees you'll hire.
- a description of what you're selling.
- a financial plan, covering how you will get the money you need to run your business, and how much you hope to make.

You should have a hard copy on paper so you can look at your business plan easily. You should also have a computer file, so you can easily change and update your business plan when you need to.

Test your filing system by challenging a friend or family member to find a certain file. If the other person can find it easily, you have a good filing system. If they can't find it quickly, rethink your filing system and change it for one that makes more sense.

Keeping Track of the Money

TAXES

All small business owners have to pay taxes on the money their businesses make, as long as they make more than $600 (for most small businesses). In addition, people have to pay taxes on the money they make themselves, which is called income tax. You will also have to pay sales tax on purchases you make in stores. The national, state, and local governments collect taxes. You might think it's unfair that the government takes the money you earned, but the government puts the taxes it collects to good use. The government uses taxes to pay for roads, parks, public schools, police, and more. You use government services every day, even to do your business. Paying for the services you use with taxes makes sense when you think about it.

Ledgers

To keep track of your money, you should also create something called a ledger. Ledgers are charts that keep track of all the things you buy for your business, and all the money you make with your business. A ledger organizes your money into one place so you can easily figure out what is going on with your business *financially*.

Ledgers are charts with a lot of rows and columns organized by date and category. Many people choose to fill out a physical ledger, but you can also fill them out on the computer.

Ledgers are really useful at *tax* time. When you have to pay taxes on your business, you are allowed to pay less tax based on how much you had to spend to run your business. You'll pay fewer taxes if you spend a lot of money on equipment, or office

Understanding Business Math & Budgets

supplies, or rent. Your business ledger can keep track of all those categories of things. Then, when you fill out your tax forms, you'll be able to easily see those numbers.

For businesses that always seem to be running out of money, ledgers help show where the business is spending too much money. If you run down the categories on your ledger and see you spent $250 on paperclips last month, you've found the problem!

Imagine you set up a ledger for your t-shirt company. So far you have bought some supplies and sold t-shirts to three customers. Your ledger could have two pages, one for supply expenses, and one for sales. Or you could just combine both sales and expenses on one ledger, which is what you choose to do. Your ledger looks like this:

Date	Description	Category	Amount	Balance
4/12	T-shirt press	Supplies	−$60	$40
4/30	2 t-shirts sold	Sales	$20	$60
5/1	Poster prints	Supplies	−$12	$48
5/1	1 t-shirt sold	Sales	$10	$58
5/2	Website domain	Supplies	−$10	$48

Your original balance, which is the amount of money you started out with, was $100. You only have $100 to spend at first, but you can spend any amount up to $100.

For the supplies, you have to subtract the price of each of the supplies you buy from the $100. You add the sales of the t-shirts to the balance, because it is additional money you are making and didn't have before. Money with a minus sign in front of the amount is money you paid to someone else. The rest is money someone paid to you.

At the end of the ledger, you see you now have $48, because that is your last balance. Your final total is a lot less than $100. But don't worry—when you start out running a business, you will have to spend a lot of money and slowly make it back as you make more and more sales.

This ledger is the simplest way to do bookkeeping. Big businesses have more **complex** ways of keeping track of money, but for now, you'll be fine with simple bookkeeping.

Computers

Computers make keeping track of money a lot easier. Check out software like Quickbooks or Quicken. Software like this guides you through the steps of bookkeeping. You don't have to know much about bookkeeping beforehand. Software can also draw graphs for you, and help you make all sorts of conclusions about how you are spending and making money.

Computer software is good for when your business grows a little more. At first, a ledger will probably be enough for you. Bookkeeping for a small business just starting out is pretty easy. Once you get several customers and really start to get going, you'll be working with more money. Then you could **invest** in some bookkeeping software.

You'll also find computers are useful for organizing some of your files. Not all of your files will be paper. Some will be files on your computer, like ads you're working on, or applications for **grants**.

Just like with your physical filing system, have a system for your computer. Keep a folder on your computer with all your electronic business records. Don't just put all your business files in one folder, though. Have more folders in your main folder for

each category of file. Have one folder for grant applications, one for your business plan, one for your advertisements, and so on. The goal is to make computer files just as easy to find as your physical files.

A Bank Account

You may have your own bank account as an individual. Many young people have savings accounts where they keep all the money they don't want to spend right away. Allowance, birthday money, and checks from jobs end up in savings accounts.

You might also have a checking account at the bank. You can take out money more easily from checking accounts. Instead of carrying around cash to pay for things, a checking account gives you a debit card and the ability to take out money from ATMs.

When you start a business, avoid using your personal bank accounts for your business. You'll quickly get confused as to what money you're saving for college or a personal computer, versus the money you set aside for your business.

Open a business bank account to keep track specifically of your business's money. Start out with a checking account, which will let you take out money to pay for business expenses. Some of the money you make from your business can go right back into the checking account to pay for more things in the future.

Just visit a local bank to set up your account. You'll need some personal identification and your business *license*. If you are under eighteen, you'll need an adult to help you open the account. People under eighteen cannot legally open an account on their own.

When you go to the store or buy something online, keep your personal and business purchases separate. Buy your personal items with cash or your personal debit card. Buy your business items with your business bankcard. You'll find it's a lot easier to separate two receipts than to figure out which items on a single receipt have to do with your business and which ones don't. Then file the business receipt in your file folders.

You'll need to keep track of the money in your business bank account too. Just like with a ledger, you can use a chart to track the money you spend with it, and the money you put into it.

Let's say you have just opened up a bank account for your t-shirt business. The person at the bank handed you a checkbook when you opened the account and told you to keep track of your money with it. You can also look at the account online, but sometimes the bank makes a mistake. You'll catch any mistakes that happen if you use the checkbook yourself.

The checkbook looks a lot like a ledger, and it uses the same math. However, ledgers keep track of all the money you spend and receive. Checkbooks only keep track of the money that goes into or out of your checking account.

Here's what your checkbook looks like, after you start selling some more t-shirts. You keep $3 from every t-shirt you sell for yourself, since you're the owner of the business. The other $7 from each t-shirt sale goes back into your business bank account.

Date	Description	Withdrawal	Deposit	Balance
5/17	4 t-shirt sales		$28	$88
5/18	ink	−$13		$75
5/30	7 t-shirt sales		$49	$124

You started out with $60 in your account. On 5/17, you took the money you made from four t-shirt sales and put it all in your account. You deposited it, which means you added it to the bank.

Understanding Business Math & Budgets

The next day, you used your debit card to buy some more ink to print t-shirts. The ink cost $23, which you withdrew—or took out—from your account. Each time you make a **transaction**, you have to do the math and come up with a new balance.

Then check your balances with what your account says online. If you see a problem, double-check your math. Then talk to the bank to see what's going on. You won't find mistakes very often, but they could happen.

TIME MATH

In a business, you will also have to keep track of time and do some time math. Business owners are often very busy, and make schedules for themselves. They decide what they need to do, how long each task will take, and when they need to do each task. If they write a schedule and then they see they have scheduled more hours than there are in a day, they haven't done the math right! When you make your own schedule, keep track of your hours and see if you are working too much or too little. You will also have to work with time math if you have employees. Your employees may be part time, and will only work so many hours every week. As the business owner and boss, you decide how many hours they work and how much they will get paid. Again, you'll need some math to figure it all out.

It takes a lot of success before any business is in the position of hiring someone dedicated to organizing their finances.

Understanding Business Math & Budgets

Accountants

Bigger businesses use accountants, who are people trained to keep track of money. When your business is small, you should figure out your *finances* yourself. You want to know what's going on with your business, and the money a small business makes and spends isn't too hard to keep track of.

But if your business grows a lot, you may want to hire someone else to keep track of the money. The bigger the business, the more confusing it gets. You'll be spending more money on lots of different things. You might have several different things you're selling. You'll be paying more taxes.

Accountants make your life simpler. They also cost money. Make sure you can afford to pay an accountant before you hire one. An accountant will be worth it, though, if you can afford it and your business grows enough.

THREE

Understanding Profit and Loss

How well your business does comes down to two numbers: profit and loss. You can also measure how well your business is doing based on how happy your customers are or how you help your community. But neither of those things will tell you whether or not you will stay in business. That's where profit

No business can make any decision without first understanding whether the decision will result in a profit or a loss.

Profit and Loss Defined

Profit is the money your business makes after you account for business expenses. Remember, it takes money to make money. The money you spend, however, takes away from your profits.

In the first two months of your t-shirt business, you sell twenty-one t-shirts. At $10 each, you made $210 total. The $210 is your revenue—the total amount of money you made from sales. However, the $210 is not your profit.

To figure out your profit, you have to see how much money you spent on your business in those two months. You spent $97 on ink, t-shirts, and advertisements. So you subtract the $97 from the $210 and get $113 as your profit. You made $113 after subtracting the money you spent.

Loss is the amount of money you have lost by doing business. If you make less money than the amount you spent to run your business, you have a loss.

Understanding Business Math & Budgets

Keeping track of costs and income is a lot of work but is a vital part of successfully running any business, small or large.

Imagine that instead of twenty-one t-shirts, you sold nine over your first two months in business. You made $90 in total.

But even though you made money, you made less than it cost you to sell the t-shirts. Since you spent $97 on supplies and advertising, you actually lost $7. If you hadn't set up your business, you wouldn't have bought those supplies and lost the $7.

However, a business loss doesn't mean your business has failed. Especially when you're just starting out, you might not make a profit or only make a very small profit. Keep an eye on things, and come up with ideas about how to make more money. Should you advertise more? Advertising usually costs money, but maybe you can be creative and advertise for free.

If your business has been around for a while and hasn't made any profits, you should rethink how you're running the business. The longer you lose money, the closer you are to closing down your business, unless you have an unlimited supply of money to pour into your business.

Profit and Loss Statements

To keep track of your profit and loss, you can make a profit-and-loss statement. These statements are summaries of how well your business is doing. You can have a profit and loss statement that covers a month, a **business quarter**, or a year. You'll be able to tell at a glance whether your business has made a profit or a loss during that time period.

Basically, a profit-and-loss statement does what we just calculated above. There are just a lot more numbers involved. You will make a lot of sales and purchases over a whole year, for example.

The key is staying organized. Keep records and receipts of all your purchases. Your file folders and computer documents will come in handy now.

To make a profit-and-loss statement, create a chart. The first part of the chart will have all of the money you made. The second part will list all of the things you paid for. At the end, subtract the totals for each section. If you get a negative number, you had a loss. If you have a positive number, you made a profit.

For example, here is what a profit and loss statement might look like after your first six months in the t-shirt business.

Income	Amount	Total
Sales	$870	
Total income		$870
Expenses		
Supplies	$238	
Business license fees	$25	
Website domain fees	$10	
Pay	$261	
Advertising	$55	
Total expenses		$589
Profit/Loss		$281

You subtracted your total expenses from your total income and found that you made a $281 profit! Not bad for your first six

Profit and loss statements can be difficult to create if a business isn't dedicated to keeping their income statements and expenses organized.

Understanding Business Math & Budgets

months. Don't forget that you paid yourself $261. The $281 represents all the money you can put back into your business to help it grow more. If you want more or less, you can choose to pay yourself more or less.

Seeing how much profit you make will show you how much your business is growing. In general, businesses start out with small profits, or even losses, and then make bigger and bigger profits. Profit and loss are some of the more useful numbers when doing business.

Understanding Profit and Loss

STARTING A BUSINESS STEP BY STEP

Starting a business can be a lot of work, but it is exciting work that will teach you a lot of things, and hopefully make you some money. Here are a few steps to starting up a serious business:

1. Decide on your business. Ask yourself what you're good at and what you enjoy doing. Can you make your interests into a business that makes you money?
2. Research your competition. Figure out if other businesses are already selling what you want to sell, and if there's room for another similar business. Take a look at what similar businesses are charging their customers to figure out your own prices.
3. Name your business. Pick a name that is creative but still tells people what your business does. Check to see the name isn't already taken by another business.
4. Officially create your business by registering it with the local or state government. Buy a business license.
5. Create a business plan. Business plans are basically roadmaps for success—they cover what your business will be, and how you will run it.
6. Make a list of your expenses. What are the things you need to buy to start your business? Will you need materials, space, employees, or training?
7. Find money. You'll need money to cover all your expenses. You can spend your own money, or find people who are willing to give you a loan.
8. Advertise. Print out flyers, advertise in the newspaper, and use the

Internet to spread the word about your business. Make sure your ads have enough information, including what you sell, how much it is, and how to contact you. Get business cards and hand them out to people you meet.

9. Keep track of finances. Write down all the money you spend and the money you make. That way, you'll be able to see if you're making money.

10. Pay taxes. If you make enough money, you legally have to pay taxes. In the United States, check with the IRS (Internal Revenue Service) to figure out if you made enough to pay taxes.

FOUR

Understanding Percentages

So far, the business math we've covered is mostly addition and subtraction. The deeper you go into business, though, the more math you'll find.

Percentages are a very useful math idea in business. People in business use percentages all the time, so it's a good idea to understand what they are and how to use them.

What Are Percentages?

Percentages are parts out of a hundred. A simple way to say 50 percent is fifty parts out of a hundred. Twenty-five percent is twenty-five parts out of a hundred.

You can write percentages in several ways, which all look a little different but mean the same thing. Often, for example, 50

SOME COMMON PERCENTAGES IN FRACTION FORM

$$100\% = \frac{1}{1}$$
$$75\% = \frac{3}{4}$$
$$50\% = \frac{1}{2}$$

$$33.33\% = \frac{1}{3}$$
$$25\% = \frac{1}{4}$$
$$10\% = \frac{1}{10}$$

percent is written 50%. You could also write 50 percent as a fraction. You could say 50/100, which means fifty parts out a hundred. You could make that fraction smaller, though. Since 100 can be divided by 50, you can divide both the numerator and the denominator by fifty. In the end, you get 50/100 = ½.

Yet another way to write the same percentage is with a deci-mal number. To **convert** a percent to a decimal number, move the decimal place in the percent two spaces to the left and take off the percent sign. So, 50% is really like saying 50.0%. Moving the decimal point to the left gives you .50. You can say .50 as "fifty hundredths," or fifty parts out of a hundred.

Understanding Business Math & Budgets

Sales give potential new customers a chance to try your product and are an important part of generating new business!

To use percentages, pick the form you want to work with. You can do percentage math with either fractions or decimals.

If you want to do percentage math, you will need to multiply. Take the number you are trying to find the percentage of, and multiply it by the fraction or decimal. You will end up with a percent of the original number. To find the percent left of the number, take the percent and subtract it from one.

Sales

One reason percentages are important in business is discounts and sales. At some point, you may want to offer customers a sale, so that they'll buy your product or service.

Sales are usually advertised as a percentage off the original price. You need to be able to calculate how much your product or

Your profit is only a percentage of all the money that your company handles on a daily basis. Percentages and fractions are two of the most basic tools for understanding how much profit your business is making.

service will be after a sale, to make sure you're not discounting it too much or too little.

At your t-shirt business, your t-shirt sales are a little slow. You decide you want to advertise a sale, which might convince some more people to buy your t-shirts. How much should you discount the shirts?

First you try 5% off. You turn the 5% into a decimal: .05. Then you multiply the $10 price by the .05 and get $.50. That's just how much the discount is. To find out the price of the t-shirt, you subtract the $.50 from $10, to end up with $9.50. You think for a little while, and decide that's not a big enough discount. If people weren't buying your shirts for $10, they probably won't buy them for $9.50.

Then you try 75% off. For this calculation, you use a fraction. To convert 75% into a fraction, you write 75/100. Then you reduce the fraction to ¾. When you multiply the price by ¾, you get $7.50. Subtracting $7.50 from $10 gives you a t-shirt price of $2.50. You think that price seems awfully low. It costs you $2 just to make the t-shirts, so you would only be making a $.50 profit.

The right discount for you is somewhere in the middle. You try out 30%. In decimal form, 30% is .30. Doing the multiplication and subtraction, you find the final price of the discounted t-shirts will be $7. That sounds about right to you, so you go ahead and advertise the sale. Sure enough, you start selling some more shirts. You just convinced some more people to buy your t-shirts with a sale!

Profits

You can also think about profits in terms of percentages. Profit percentages are called profit *margins*. They are given in terms of profits per cost of producing what you're selling.

Some loans have higher interest rates than others. Percentages help you understand how much interest you will be paying on a loan.

You can look at profit margins for periods of time. Let's go back to the example of your first six months. You spent $589 to produce everything you sold. Your profits were $281 in those same six months.

To find the profit margin, just divide your profit by the costs. So $281/$589 is about .48, or 48%.

Normal profit margins are about 20 to 30 percent. Anything less, and you should be trying to figure out how to make more profit. Anything more, and you're doing really good business. It turns out that your t-shirt business is making you a lot of money, if you think about it in terms of profit margins!

Loans

Someday you may need a loan from the bank. Loans are like borrowing money from the bank. When you borrow money from your family or friends, you probably just pay them back the amount you borrowed. When you borrow from a bank, you have to pay back the original amount, plus more money called interest.

Interest is basically the **fee** you pay for being able to borrow the money from the bank. The bank makes money by lending people money. Interest is given in percentages.

Your bank may charge you two kinds of interest. The first is called simple interest. Simple interest is an amount of money paid only on what you borrowed in the first place.

The equation for simple interest is:

$$I = prt$$

Where I is the total interest you'll pay, p is the principal (or the amount of money loaned to you), r is the interest *rate*, and t is time in years you have to pay the loan back.

Interest is always a percent. To fill out the equation, though, you'll need to turn the percent into a decimal number.

Let's say you want to take a loan out of the bank for your business. You need $3,000 to buy a really nice, new t-shirt press, and maybe hire an employee. You don't have $3,000 to spend, but you might if you could get the press and sell lots more t-shirts. Then you could pay the $3,000 back in the future. However, you'll end up paying more than $3,000 because of interest.

You go to the bank and find out the interest rate is 6.5 percent. You have two years to pay back the loan. To figure out how much you'll have to pay, plug in all the numbers you have into the simple interest equation:

$$I = \$3,000 \times .065 \times 2$$
$$I = \$390$$

What that means is that you will have to pay the bank $390 in interest, or $3,390 in total over two years.

Most of the time, the bank will not charge simple interest. They will charge **compound** interest. Compound interest is basically like interest on interest. First, the original amount you borrowed will earn some interest. The next time interest is added, it will be a percentage of the original amount you borrowed, plus the first interest. You end up paying a lot more interest this way.

Here is the equation for compound interest:

$$S = P (1 + r/n)^{nt}$$

Where S is the future total value of what you'll need to pay the bank, P is the principal (amount you originally borrowed), r is the interest rate in decimal form, n is the number of times per year the interest is added, and t is the time in years you have to pay the loan back.

The n and the t are set as small characters because they are exponents. Exponents tell you how many times you multiply a number by itself. For example, 3^2 equals 3 times 3, or 9. And 3^3 is 3 times 3 times 3, or 27. Your calculator or computer will be able to calculate exponents for you.

For the same bank loan with compound interest added monthly:

$$S = \$3{,}000(1 + .065/12)^{12 \times 2}$$
$$S = \$3415.29$$

You can see you'll pay more money with compound interest. Banks pretty much always only offer compound interest loans, rather than simple interest loans.

Savings Accounts

If you have opened a business savings account at the bank, you will also have to think about interest. But this time, you are earning interest, not paying it!

The bank adds interest to your savings accounts, so you might notice a monthly interest payment in your account balance.

The interest you make is usually compound interest. You can use the same compound interest equation as before to figure out how much interest you'll make on the money in your savings account.

If you have $567 in your savings account, you'll make some money on it over a year. The interest rate is 1% and it is added once a month:

$$S = P(1 + r/n)^{nt}$$
$$S = \$567(1 + .01/12)^{12 \times 1}$$

Understanding Percentages

$$P = \left(1 + \frac{r}{n}\right)^{nt}$$

Calculating the interest that you will be making from your investments can help you plan for the future!

Understanding Business Math & Budgets

S= $572.70

In other words, you'll make $5.70 in interest. The amount may not be a lot, but it's more than nothing! And the more you keep in your savings account, the more interest you'll earn.

FIVE

Making a Budget

*B*udgets are another big tool you should use to organize your business and keep track of your money with numbers and math. Successful businesses have budgets, which help them see how much money they have to spend and guides spending decisions.

A budget is a plan. You could decide not to create a budget, but then you'd just be spending your business's money whenever you wanted. If you wanted to hire an employee, you would just hire someone and start paying her, even if your business didn't really have enough money. With a budget, you can look to see if your business can afford to hire an employee, and if it can, how much she should be paid and how many hours she should work.

Budgets aren't too hard to make. They're worth the time and effort, too, because you'll have a clearer idea about what is happening in your business.

When and Where

Budgets used to be written down on paper. Some people still make budget charts by hand. Most businesses now use computer software or Excel to create a budget, but you can do whatever makes more sense to you. Be sure to keep your budgets either in a file folder or an organized computer folder. The best idea is to keep it in both.

You may want to create a budget for each month you're in business. That way, you'll have a plan for spending money month to month. Budgets for entire years are harder to follow. You don't really know how much money you'll make or need to spend months from now.

Parts of a Budget

The information you include in a budget might look familiar. You include sales and other *revenue*, along with expenses. You're using the same numbers as when you came up with your profits. Revenues and expenses are some of the most important numbers when it comes to business.

The expenses on a budget are broken down into a few categories. First, you have "fixed expenses." Your fixed expenses stay the same, no matter how many sales you make. If you rented a store, for example, you would have to pay rent every month no matter what.

Variable expenses change with how many products you make. Each product you make or service you provide costs some amount of money. The more products or services you make, the more you spend (but also the more money you make in sales). They are called variable expenses because they vary with time and production.

How to Put a Budget Together

The very first time you make a budget you'll have to make some pretty rough guesses. You don't really know how much you'll need to spend or how much you'll make. Do your best to make good guesses.

After that, budgets get easier. You can base your next budget off the one that came before it. You have a better idea of your expenses and sales.

The first budget you create for your t-shirt business is for the first month you're in business. You haven't sold anything yet, so you don't really know what numbers to use.

Your first budget will look something like this:

Category	Budgeted	Actual	Difference
Fixed Expenses			
T-shirt press	$60	$60	$0
Advertising	$12	$12	$0
Pay	$15	$12	−$3
Variable Expenses			
T-shirts	$15	$10	+$5
Ink	$30	$23	+$7
Total for Expenses	$135	$117	+$18

Category	Budgeted	Actual	Difference
Revenue			
Sales	$50	$40	−$10
Total for Revenue	$50	$40	−$10

You know how much the t-shirt press was, because you already bought it. You also know you want to pay yourself $3 from every $10 shirt, but you don't know how many shirts you'll sell. You have to guess that number, and your revenue from t-shirt sales. You're also not entirely sure how many t-shirts one bottle of ink will print, so you guess the ink expense too.

Your budgeted expenses are also based on how much money you have to spend. If you only have $20 this month to buy t-shirts, you will budget $20 for t-shirts. You can't spend any more than that, or your business will start losing money.

You'll notice the actual amounts you spent and made are a little different than what you budgeted. That's okay, because you were just making some good guesses.

The "difference" column is very important. The negative numbers mean you actually spent more or earned less than you thought you would. The positive numbers mean you spent less or earned more than you guessed. For the next month's budget, try to get the difference as close to zero as possible.

For the next month's budget, now you have a better idea of what numbers to use. You can also assume you'll sell a few more t-shirts because you have been advertising.

You'll get better and better at budgets over time. The goal isn't necessarily to be exact, but to have a good idea of how much money you will have to spend and then stick to the budget. You'll also start seeing if you make more money than expected, and can spend more to keep the business growing.

You might want to spend more money on advertising, for example. Do you have enough money in your budget? If you keep selling more t-shirts than you budget for, you have the **funds** to spend on more advertising. Budgets help you make good business decisions.

MORE BUSINESS IDEAS

Young people can start all kinds of businesses. You just need some imagination and hard work, and you can run a successful business. The possibilities depend on you—what you are good at and like to do.

- Lawn care: Mow lawns, shovel snow, rake leaves, and plant gardens, depending on the season and where you live.
- Errands: Offer to help people who can't get around or who don't have enough time by grocery shopping, picking up things from the drug store, and taking letters to the post office.
- Crafts: Make jewelry, knit scarves, or create pottery to sell at craft shows, at local stores, or online.
- Create a computer or phone application: If you're technologically savvy, create games or other applications for computers and smartphones.
- Babysitter or petsitter: Watch other people's children or pets.
- Dog walker: Walk neighbors' dogs.
- Tutor: Teach people math, English, history, computers, and more, depending on what you're good at.

Making a Budget

No matter what kind of business you run, making a budget will help you pay back loans and protect investments.

Understanding Business Math & Budgets

Lemonade Stand Math

One organization, called Lemonade Day, is bringing business math and knowledge to young people around the country. Lemonade Day has spread to many states all around the country. Participants in Lemonade Day learn how to set up a business, and compete with each other to see who can run the best lemonade stand.

Participants learn a lot about budgeting and other kinds of business math. Take Lanandi Addison, for example, a participant from Washington, D.C. Lanandi's dream is to open a skateboard shop someday, so she wanted to learn more about business.

For Lemonade Day, Lanandi asked around for money to borrow. She ended up with a $75 loan from her father, which she had to pay back.

Another Washington, D.C. student named Lloyd also borrowed some money, from his mother. He eventually decided he would pay his mother back with 5 percent interest.

Lanandi and other participants also learned why budgets were important, and created their own budgets. She said, "You have to plan and budget your money so nothing will mess you up. If a problem occurs, you need to have a back-up plan."

Then there is Clayton, a fifth grader from Indiana who has participated in Lemonade Day three years in a row. Clayton has had some pretty great lemonade stands, including a circus-themed stand.

Clayton's experiences have taught him about things like bank accounts and profits. He says, "Last year I had planned to use some of my money to spend on a tablet. But because I won an iPad® at the best stand contest, I put all of my spend and save

Lemonade Day participants are encouraged to give back to their communities. Like any good business, they do more than make a profit!

money in my savings account." Then he adds, "I chose to share 20 percent of my profits with a special needs camp in Indiana in honor of my friend Emily who has Down's syndrome." Clayton knew how much he made in profits, and then he could calculate 20 percent out to give to charity.

Lemonade Day participants are learning that it pays to pay attention to math in business. Each stand ends up bringing in an average of $100 in profit.

Understanding Business Math & Budgets

Budgets, profit and loss statements, ledgers, and more are all great methods of keeping track of your business's money. They all use math, from addition and subtraction to percentages. And well-run businesses based on math are successful businesses. Business math will help you build a strong business!

Find Out More

ONLINE

Budget Worksheets
www.moneyandstuff.info/budgetworksheet.htm

Compounding Calculator
www.themint.org/kids/compounding-calculator.html

It All Adds Up
www.italladdsup.org

Lemonade Day
www.lemonadeday.org

Teaching Kids Business: Finance
www.teachingkidsbusiness.com/business-basics-finance.htm

IN BOOKS

Benjamin, Arthur and Michael Shermer. *Secrets of Mental Math.* New York: Three Rivers Press, 2006.

Bernstein, Daryl. *Better Than a Lemonade Stand! Small Business Ideas for Kids.* New York: Aladdin, 2012.

Chatzky, Jean. *Not Your Parents' Money Book.* New York: Simon and Schuster, 2010.

Mooney, Carla. *Starting a Business: Have Fun and Make Money.* Chicago, Ill.: Norwood House Press, 2010.

Walsh, Kieran. *Money Math.* Vero Beach, Fla.: Rourke Publishing, 2004.

Vocabulary

Business quarter: a unit of time that a business uses to calculate profits and losses; each year has four quarters called Q1, Q2, Q3, and Q4.

Compound: determining interest based on both the principal (the beginning amount) and the additional interest payments as they are added on to the principal.

Convert: to change.

Expense: money spent.

Fee: money paid for the use of a service.

Finances: the management of money.

Financially: having to do with money.

Funds: money saved for a particular purpose.

Grants: money given away by a government or company for a specific purpose.

Invest: to use money in expectation of making some money from it in the future.

License: a written legal permission to do something.

Margins: an amount by which something increases or decreases.

Rate: the speed at which something happens.

Receipts: written statements that a purchase has been made.

Revenue: income, money made.

Tax: money collected by a government to pay for services such as roads, schools, and parks.

Transaction: one instance of buying or selling something.

Unit price: how much something costs per certain amount such as pound or ounce.

Index

About the Author and Consultant

Helen Thompson lives in upstate New York. She worked first as a social worker and then became a teacher as her second career.

Brigitte Madrian is the Aetna Professor of Public Policy and Corporate Management at the Harvard Kennedy School. Before coming to Harvard in 2006, she was on the faculty at the University of Pennsylvania Wharton School (2003–2006), the University of Chicago Graduate School of Business (1995–2003) and the Harvard University Economics Department (1993–1995). She is also a research associate and co-director of the Household Finance working group at the National Bureau of Economic Research. Dr. Madrian received her PhD in economics from the Massachusetts Institute of Technology and studied economics as an undergraduate at Brigham Young University. She is the recipient of the National Academy of Social Insurance Dissertation Prize (first place, 1994) and a two-time recipient of the TIAA-CREF Paul A. Samuelson Award for Scholarly Research on Lifelong Financial Security (2002 and 2011).

Picture Credits